Horses!

Horse Rescue

Katie Marsico

Cavendish
Square

New York

Published in 2014 by Cavendish Square Publishing, LLC
303 Park Avenue South, Suite 1247, New York, NY 10010

Copyright © 2014 by Cavendish Square Publishing, LLC

First Edition

Website: cavendishsq.com

CPSIA Compliance Information: Batch #WS13CSQ

All websites were available and accurate when this book was sent to press.

Library of Congress Cataloging-in-Publication Data
Marsico, Katie, 1980–
Horse rescue / Katie Marsico.
p. cm. — (Horses!)
Includes bibliographical references and index.
Summary: "Provides comprehensive information on the rescue of abandoned horses"—Provided by publisher.
ISBN 978-1-60870-836-9 (hardcover)   ISBN 978-1-62712-086-9 (paperback)   ISBN 978-1-60870-842-0 (ebook)
1. Horses—Juvenile literature. 2. Animal rescue—Juvenile literature. 3. Animal welfare—Juvenile literature. I. Title.
HV4749.M37 2013
636.08'32—DC32
2011037911

Editor: Christine Florie
Art Director: Anahid Hamparian
Series Designer: Virginia Pope

Expert Reader: United States Equine Rescue League, Inc., Raleigh, North Carolina

Photo research by Marybeth Kavanagh

Cover photo by Sanford Myers/The Tennessean/AP Photo

The photographs in this book are used by permission and through the courtesy of: *Alamy:* Mark J. Barrett, 4, 28; The Protected Art Archive, 8; Tim Graham, 10; Matthew Renwick, 15; LOOK Die Bildagentur der Fotografen GmbH, 31; *The Granger Collection, New York:* 7; *AP Photo:* The Florida Times-Union/Terry Dickson, 9; Laura Rauch, 18; The Daily Times/Todd G. Dudek, 20, 40; The Oklahoman/Chris Landsberger, 22; *Getty Images:* Peter Anderson/Dorling Kindersley, 12; Al Diaz/Miami Herald/MCT, 34; *Newscom:* Jason Szenes/EPA, 16; ZUMA Press, 24; *SuperStock:* Mindbodysoul, 25; Nomad, 27; Don White, 33; *Beth Hyman/SquirrelWood Equine Sanctuary,* 38

Printed in the United States of America

Contents

One

A Second Chance at Survival

What do you picture when you think about horses? Maybe you imagine a powerful champion speeding toward the finish line on a racetrack. Perhaps you have a vision of a carriage horse proudly pulling a coach or a friendly pony giving rides to children on a farm. All of these images involve animals that are both graceful and amazing. But what happens when owners can no longer keep their horses or use them to race or work?

Sadly, many horses end up being **euthanized** or shipped to a **slaughterhouse** to die. Other horses suffer neglect or abuse when their owners cannot care for them or do not see them as useful anymore. Luckily, some unwanted horses enjoy a happier ending. Rescues and **sanctuaries** take in horses that have been abandoned or are headed to their deaths. These organizations provide food, shelter, veterinary care, and most important, a second chance at life.

← Rescued horses roam the pastures at Proud Spirit
Horse Sanctuary in Mena, Arkansas.

Sent to Slaughter

Many lawmakers are fighting to keep horses from being slaughtered in the United States. Yet this does not mean that unwanted horses are safe. Dealers who buy horses for slaughter often work beyond U.S. boundaries. They ship horses to countries such as Canada and Mexico. Slaughterhouses there kill the animals to sell their meat and to make other products.

A History of Helping Horses

Horse rescue dates back hundreds of years. In the 1800s Americans began paying closer attention to how horses were being treated. During that time period, people still relied on horses to pull everything from carriages to farm and factory machinery. They also watched horses perform in circuses and races. People used horses to get several different jobs done and to move across the growing country. Horses helped them do work and provided them with entertainment.

Yet this did not mean that people always treated their animals well. It was not unusual to see horses being beaten or starved. Many people saw horses mainly as tools rather than as living creatures. Horses that were too old or sick to do their jobs were often killed and replaced without a second thought.

This situation began to change in the nineteenth century. The American Society for the Prevention of Cruelty to Animals (ASPCA), founded by Henry Bergh, opened in New York City in 1866. This organization was formed to help protect animals such as horses from unkind and dangerous treatment. By the 1880s the first horse rescue opened near Philadelphia, Pennsylvania. Workers there took in and cared for old and abused horses. More than 130 years later, hundreds of rescues and sanctuaries exist across the United States.

Henry Bergh, founder of the ASPCA, inspects a horse pulling an overcrowded streetcar.

Rescues versus Sanctuaries

It is important to understand that not all rescues and sanctuaries work the same way. For starters, the terms *rescue* and *sanctuary* can mean different things. In most cases, a horse that is taken in by a rescue is **rehabilitated** until it is ready to be adopted by new owners. Meanwhile, a sanctuary is often willing to let an unwanted animal live there for the rest of its life.

Read about How Horses Feel!

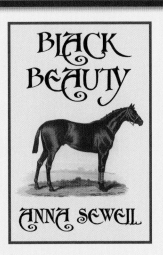

Have you ever heard of the book *Black Beauty*? This novel, written by a woman from England named Anna Sewell, was published in 1877. It tells the story of a horse named Black Beauty from the animal's point of view. Black Beauty has a difficult life as he passes from owner to owner and works pulling coaches in England. Along the way, Black Beauty tells readers about how different people treat him and how it makes him feel.

This unique story came at an important time in horse-rescue work. Not long after *Black Beauty* was published, more rescues and sanctuaries started forming in the United States. The book made readers everywhere more aware of how horses should be treated and why they need people's help.

Why do certain horses head to rescues while others go to sanctuaries? Sometimes it just depends on which group is ready and willing to take an animal in after it has been rescued. Rescuers usually also try to think about which setting will work best for a particular horse over a long period of time.

Apache is a rehabilitated horse that was adopted through a rescue program in Georgia.

For example, a horse that has been given up because of an injury that limits its speed may still be able to enjoy a good life with a new owner who is not interested in racing. In this case, the animal might be a good fit at a rescue that can rehabilitate the horse and help find the right person to adopt it.

Yet not every rescued horse would do well being placed in a new home. Some horses need special medical care that owners might find hard to provide. Other horses have been severely abused or neglected and are too nervous to be ridden or handled. These horses often do best at a sanctuary, where they can spend the rest of their lives in one safe place.

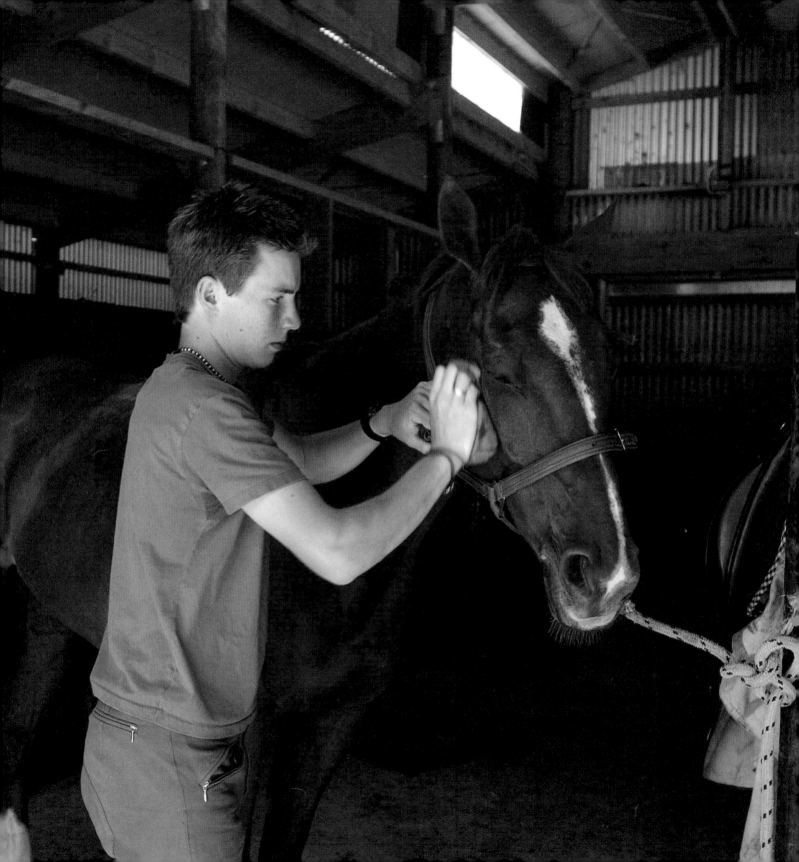

Two

Different Horses That Are Helped

You might be asking yourself why anyone would ever give up a horse. Even horses that can no longer race or pull heavy loads can still live long, healthy lives. Many of these animals are friendly and can be easily ridden and handled. They make excellent pets on a farm or ranch.

Not everyone who gives up a horse is cruel or irresponsible. Some people simply have no idea what they are getting into when they buy a horse. Horses can live anywhere from twenty to thirty years. This means that owners must be prepared to care for them much longer than they would care for a dog, cat, or other pet.

What many people do not realize is how expensive owning a horse for twenty to thirty years actually is. It can cost several thousand dollars to feed and house a single horse for just one year! The price rises even more when you add in fees such as veterinary care or any kind of special training.

← Owning a horse is a long-term commitment that involves
   a great deal of time and money.

Caring for a horse is expensive. Feeding one horse costs more than $1,000 per year.

Some people are also unaware of all the responsibilities that go into owning a horse. Horses need to be **groomed** and must have regular checkups with a veterinarian. They also need enough space to move around comfortably and to exercise. Horses are large animals that cannot simply be kept in a person's small backyard. People who do not own enough land to house a horse must therefore pay for boarding at a nearby stable.

Some people *do* know what is involved in caring for a horse, but then changes in their lives make it difficult to keep their animals. Owners who get sick or lose their jobs sometimes face tough choices when it comes to their horses. Many must deal with the sad realization that they do not have the time or money to continue caring for their animals.

People often try to do the right thing by finding their horses new homes. Sometimes their efforts lead to a happy ending. This is not always the case, though. Some horses fall into the wrong hands. People who are desperate to make money or to get rid of their horses risk selling them to someone they do not know very well. In these situations, new owners may be even less fit to care for the animal than the previous owner was!

There are also people who do not even bother to search for new homes for their horses. These owners may simply stop looking after their animals or completely abandon them. Others try to care for their horses but do not have the time or money to do it the right way. This can cause horses to get sick and sometimes even to die.

Too Old or Injured to Work

Not everyone gets rid of horses for the same reasons. Some people decide they no longer want to keep their horses once the animals become too old or injured to do a certain job. Racehorses are a common example of this.

Keep in mind that many racehorses run at the track for only a few years. During this time some horses receive serious injuries that affect their speed and movement for the rest of their lives. Some owners choose to care for their horses until the day they die. Yet others see their animals mainly as a way of earning money. A horse that is too sick or too old to run loses its value to these owners.

Sometimes the best solution for owners who do not wish to keep their racehorses is to find their animals loving homes. In other cases, the answer is to research rescues and sanctuaries and find one that takes unwanted racehorses. Yet not all owners take the time to do either of these things.

Some owners ask a vet to euthanize their horses even if the animals are still young and healthy. Others **auction** off their animals to the highest bidder—regardless of whether or not that person will take good care of a horse. It is not unusual for such horses to be at risk of abuse or neglect. They may end up leaving the auction block just to head straight to a slaughterhouse.

Unwanted racehorses are not the only horses to face this risk. Working horses such as draft horses often do as well. Draft horses are used to pull heavy loads such as carts or plows. Yet injuries and old age limit how long

When a racehorse is past its prime, some owners decide to give it up.

The Realities of Racehorses

About 35,000 Thoroughbred horses are born in the United States every year. Thoroughbred horses are pure-bred animals that are often used for racing. Experts believe that of the 35,000 Thoroughbreds born yearly, roughly 23,800 become racehorses.

Yet their careers do not last long. About three thousand race-horses leave the track every year. Most of them retire by the age of six. Experts also say that two out of three former racehorses are euthanized, abandoned, or slaughtered. Many of these horses are young and healthy, but they are not given the chance to find new homes.

they are able to work. This leaves many draft horses dealing with the same unhealthy and dangerous situations as unwanted racehorses do.

Any horse that people use to do a certain job faces an uncertain future once it is no longer able to work. Horses that pull carriages or give rides at carnivals are a few more examples of animals that sometimes end up at rescues and sanctuaries. These lucky horses are given a second chance—even if they are not as young, fast, or strong as they used to be.

Without Protection in the Wild

Some horses spend little or no time with people before they head to rescues or sanctuaries. This is true for many of the wild mustangs and burros that live throughout the American Southwest. Mustangs and burros need protection because certain ranchers see them as a threat.

Wild horses roam lands that ranchers like to use for **grazing** cattle and other farm animals. The ranchers want the government to let them round up mustangs and burros and auction them off to private owners. These wild horses often end up in holding areas where they are at risk of being shipped off to slaughterhouses. At the very least, it is not uncommon for such mustangs and burros to experience distress as they are forced into captivity after living in the wild. They are not used to being handled by people or being separated from other members of their **herd**. These horses are also at risk of catching illnesses they never were exposed to in the wild.

A herd of wild horses is held in temporary pens in Nevada. They will either be adopted or be sent to sanctuaries.

Rescues and sanctuaries that take mustangs and burros give them a safe place to live and to roam. In many cases, they care for the animals for the rest of their lives. Most rescues and sanctuaries try to create a natural setting for the wild horses. The people who run these organizations are against the idea that mustangs and burros should be locked in **corrals** and

What Is Happening to Wild Horses?

Exactly how many wild mustangs and burros have been removed from the lands they once roamed? The Humane Society of the United States (HSUS) says that the answer is close to 74,000 animals over the past ten years. The HSUS also says that the U.S. government plans to remove about 15,000 more of the animals in 2011 and 2012.

Some people see no harm in the capturing and selling of wild mustangs and burros. Yet others believe it is cruel to separate the animals from other members of their herd and keep them captive. They also argue that it is unfair to force them off land simply so that farmers and ranchers can use it for grazing. Finally, many people who are against trapping and selling mustangs and burros point out that these wild horses end up being sold for slaughter.

holding pens. They want to give the horses a second chance to enjoy the freedom of living in open spaces and belonging to a wild herd.

Three

From Danger to a Fresh Start

How exactly are horses rescued? There are several different answers to that question. Some rescues and sanctuaries get horses directly from their original owners. Rescue workers and volunteers may visit racetracks, draft stables, and farms to help unwanted animals.

Other rescues and sanctuaries find horses at auctions. In many cases, workers and volunteers try to outbid "kill" buyers who plan on slaughtering the horses. Sometimes rescues and sanctuaries purchase the horses from these buyers after the auction is over.

There are also situations where horses are rescued from **feedlots**, or kill pens. Horses are kept in these areas just before they are sent to be slaughtered. It is important to keep in mind that rescuing costs money. At the very least, rescues and sanctuaries must often pay for horses to be transported and nursed back to health.

← Goliath and a rescue volunteer enjoy their ride at Whimsical Equine Rescue in Delaware.

This neglected horse was seized by an Oklahoma county sheriff and brought to Blaze's Tribute Equine Rescue.

In a lot of cases, rescue organizations must use money to buy the horses themselves. Some owners simply give unwanted horses to rescues and sanctuaries, yet it is not uncommon for them to sell horses, too. Owners usually want to make at least some money from animals that they originally bought to race or work. Remember that rescues and sanctuaries must also pay money to outbid other buyers at auctions or to purchase horses from dealers who plan on slaughtering them.

Right after Being Rescued

The situations you have just read about are only part of the journey that many horses experience as they begin new lives at rescues and sanctuaries. Different organizations work in different ways, yet most follow a few similar steps after taking in a rescued horse. Beth Hyman is the president of

Lives Sold for Much Lower Prices

How much does it cost to buy a racehorse? The answer depends on when the animal is up for sale. Prices at the beginning of a horse's racing career are usually much higher than they are when the horse is no longer wanted on the track. For example, a Maryland woman named Laura Ann Mullane mentioned in an article in the *Washington Post* that she bought a former racehorse that originally sold for $75,000. The price dropped to $650 when the horse was resold at an auction three years later. Mullane described how the horse looked when she bought him on the auction block:

> *"By then he was 200 pounds underweight," she noted. "His ribs poked through a patchy coat that was riddled [filled] with scabs from a skin infection called rain rot. His hooves were the equivalent [equal] of tires with their treads worn bare. He had run twenty-one races—never winning a single one*

SquirrelWood Equine Sanctuary in Montgomery, New York. She describes what usually happens at her sanctuary after a new horse arrives.

"Horses are first brought to our **quarantine** area," Hyman explains. Horses that are quarantined are kept separate from other animals. Many rescues and organizations do this to make sure that the new horses are healthy and that they will not spread any illnesses or diseases. "We check the horses when they come in," continues Hyman. "We see how they are breathing and take their temperature. We also pay attention to their heart rate. The horses are carefully examined for signs of injury or illness."

Hyman says that the quarantine process at her sanctuary is strict. Whoever is near a new horse must wear special boots, gloves, and gowns. The horse stays in its own **paddock** or barn and must always be kept 40 feet away from other animals at the sanctuary. If a new horse is healthy, it is quarantined for only thirty days. If it is unhealthy, it must stay separated for another thirty days from the last time it showed any signs of illness.

Rescues quarantine newcomers before they are introduced to the general population.

Becoming Aware of a Horse's Behavior

Hyman and the other workers at SquirrelWood study many parts of a rescued horse's behavior to decide if it is ready for adoption. For starters, they check to see if a horse stays calm when a person approaches it. Next, Hyman and her workers find out if the animal lets people touch its feet, head, ears, and tail. Then they see if the horse stands when they ask it to. Hyman and her team also try to figure out if the horse will let someone lead it around the stable. Finally, they see if they can clean the horse's living space without it getting anxious.

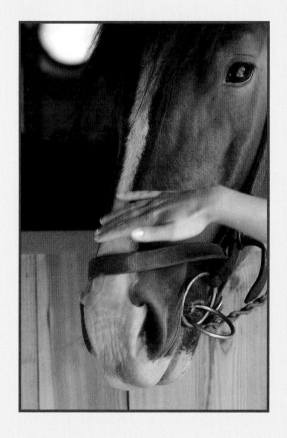

If a horse passes all these tests, Hyman tries additional activities such as grooming and bathing. Eventually she checks how the horse reacts to being ridden. These tests help the workers at SquirrelWood learn how much training a horse may need and when it might be ready for a new home.

Hyman explains that rescued horses were often in contact with sick animals. She says this is especially true for horses rescued at auctions and feedlots. It is not uncommon for these animals to be packed into a small area where they are nose to nose with other horses. These conditions, plus the stress of traveling back and forth, put the horses at risk of becoming ill. Most rescues and sanctuaries work with veterinarians who help treat any sick horses. Once their quarantine is over, the horses are ready to spend more time with the workers and volunteers who have rescued them.

Getting to Know New Horses

At SquirrelWood the end of a new horse's quarantine period is a chance to get to know the animal better. Hyman says that she and other sanctuary workers are usually already familiar with the horse. Yet she explains that everything becomes much more "hands-on" once the quarantine is over.

"At this point the horses are groomed and bathed," Hyman says. "They also get vaccinations." Vaccinations are shots that stop the horses from catching any new illnesses. Hyman mentions that the horses at her sanctuary usually see a farrier as well. A farrier is a worker who trims the horses' hooves and fits them for horseshoes.

Other rescues and sanctuaries may try to figure out whether a horse needs any particular kind of rehabilitation. It is not unusual for rescued racehorses and working horses to arrive with untreated injuries. This is because their owners sometimes give them medicines that make their pain go away, yet these medicines do not always treat the injuries themselves. The drugs simply allow the horses to keep running or working.

Horses are groomed upon arriving at a sanctuary.

Not giving an animal the time and treatment that are needed to heal an injury can make the problem worse. Some horses that have experienced this must be rehabilitated so that they do not become **lame** for life. Veterinarians and the workers at rescues and sanctuaries work closely with their horses to choose the best ways to help the animals get better.

Hyman explains that it is also important to study how any rescued horse acts when it is around people. "We ask ourselves the following questions," she says. "Is the horse nervous or jumpy? Can it be ridden without acting up?" Rescue and sanctuary workers must be able to figure out the answers to these questions. This will help them make a decision about what the future of the rescued horse should be.

Four

Figuring Out a Horse's Future

Not all rescued horses share the same future. This is because each one has a completely different story. They all experienced different lives before ending up at a rescue or sanctuary. Beth Hyman of SquirrelWood Equine Sanctuary says that the horses she works with are proof of this fact. She explains that some rescued horses take no time at all before they are ready to move on to a new home.

"The main thing that decides a horse's future is its behavior," Hyman says. "Horses that are calm and well trained can usually be put up for adoption. Many of the horses we get are perfectly behaved and can do great in a new home."

Yet it is important for rescues and sanctuaries to be sure that whoever is adopting a rescued horse is ready for the responsibility of caring for it. No one wants a horse to fall into the wrong hands or to end up with a

← People who work with rescued horses must put thought, time, and effort into deciding their futures.

person who plans on selling it for slaughter or any other reason. Most horses that make their way to rescues and sanctuaries have already been through several changes and difficulties. Workers and volunteers want to be certain that these animals go to new owners who will give them loving homes for the rest of their lives.

Working Their Way toward New Homes

It takes some horses longer than others to make their way to new homes. It is important not to rush a rescued horse into an adoption before it is ready.

Not Just Any New Owner

Most rescues and sanctuaries that put horses up for adoption **screen** owners. They ask potential owners about their experience with horses. Many rescues and sanctuaries visit the candidates' homes to see where a new horse will be living. Hyman says that her sanctuary takes things a step further. She and other workers keep an eye on horses even after their new owners have adopted them.

"The horses that come through here are followed and checked on once they leave," Hyman explains. "We can do unannounced checks and can take a rescued animal back if there are signs of neglect or mistreatment. Most of our horses do find wonderful homes, though!"

This can lead to the horse having problems with its new owner. Most of these problems usually have to do with how a horse behaves.

Horses that have been abused or neglected might be nervous or **aggressive**. They may need extra time to get used to trusting people again. Rescues and sanctuaries that put horses up for adoption understand that helping the horses deal with these issues through time gives them a better chance of finding new homes.

It takes some rescued horses a while before they learn to trust people again.

In other cases, horses struggle with physical problems that affect their chances of being adopted. Many times these problems can be fixed with rest and proper treatment from a veterinarian. The goal of rehabilitation is usually not to make rescued horses well enough to race or to work again. Yet rescues and sanctuaries want their animals to be as comfortable as possible. The fewer medical problems a horse is struggling with, the less money a new owner will have to spend on the horse's care.

The Cost of Caring for a Rescued Horse

How much does it cost rescues and sanctuaries to keep a horse for the rest of its life? A lot depends on the kind of medical treatment and training that the animal needs. Hyman notes that caring for one of the horses that will live at SquirrelWood for the rest of its life costs anywhere from $200 to $400 a month.

When Adoption Is Not an Option

If a rescued horse does not get adopted, it can still have an enjoyable life. Hyman explains that some animals simply do not have good chances of finding new homes after they arrive at her sanctuary. She says that there are many reasons that this happens, and some of these reasons also explain why certain dogs and cats do not get adopted from shelters.

"Age plays a role," Hyman notes. "An old horse is far less likely to get adopted than a young one. Kind of like shelter dogs—the old . . . just do not get homes [as often]. Horses with lameness . . . usually end up staying at sanctuaries because people . . . do not want a horse they cannot ride."

It is also challenging to find new homes for rescued horses that have serious behavioral problems. Some have been so severely abused or neglected that they will never learn to trust most people again. Sending these horses into new homes would be difficult for both them and their new owners. It would also probably lead to the horses' being returned to the rescues or sanctuaries from which they were adopted.

Older horses are often more difficult to place than young ones.

The animals in these challenging situations usually do best spending the rest of their lives in the same place. These horses need to be in a place where people will be patient with the way they act or the physical problems they are dealing with. Hyman says that her sanctuary and others like it are able to give rescued horses this type of lifelong care.

"When we rescue a horse from an auction we plan on having to care for that horse for life," Hyman explains. "There is no guarantee that a horse will be placed. We know that a small handful of our horses will have either severe behavioral issues or physical problems that will place them in our sanctuary forever."

Five

Real Stories of Rescued Horses

Every rescued horse has a unique life story. Each one has lived out a different past before entering a rescue or sanctuary. These horses also have different futures after getting a second chance at survival. The stories of two horses named Abraham and Parchita are examples of the amazing— and often opposite—paths that rescued horses' lives can take.

Abraham, or Abe, is a plow horse. When he was young and strong he pulled farm equipment in his owners' fields. Yet Abe's hard work was not enough to make them want to keep him as he grew old and sick.

The farmers who used Abe in their fields decided it was time to sell him at an auction in New Holland, Pennsylvania, in early winter 2008. The dealer who bought him planned to send him straight to a slaughterhouse. Many of the buyers who looked at Abe found it hard to imagine what else he might be good for. He was extremely underweight and had

← A young girl pets a horse at a rescue center in Florida.

an illness called canker that was causing his hooves to rot right off his feet. Abe was also suffering from heart problems that made it difficult for him to keep pulling heavy farm machinery in the fields. Finally, he was more than twenty years old. So who would want to adopt Abe or give him a second chance at life?

Extra Care for Older Animals

Older rescued horses may be harder to put up for adoption. Yet that does not mean that rescues and sanctuaries are not looking out for them. In fact, some organizations take in only older horses. Groups that do this kind of work try to provide older horses with the extra care they need later in life.

For instance, younger horses need to have a dental checkup only about once a year. Older horses, however, usually need to have their teeth checked twice as often. Teeth that are too sharp can make it difficult for them to eat. Older horses also often have to eat special foods that are easy for them to digest. These are just a few examples of how rescues and sanctuaries put extra time and effort into caring for their older animals.

Beth Hyman helped answer that question. A different rescue bought Abe from the dealer who planned to kill him and eventually brought him to SquirrelWood. Hyman describes how they cared for Abe shortly after he arrived.

"We fed him the best alfalfa we could find and slowly started him back on [a diet of] grain," she says. "His feet were cleaned and dressed daily while we fought the canker. Each day he looked at us with his huge brown eyes with a mix of curiosity and sadness. He had been through so much and did not really trust people anymore." Hyman knew that she would never be able to place Abe in a new home. His age, health problems, and trust issues simply did not make adoption a possibility. However, he would be able to spend the rest of his life at the sanctuary—which is where he is today.

As a few months passed, Abe began to get more comfortable at SquirrelWood. He started searching workers' pockets for cookies. He even "adopted" another rescued horse named Pesto. Abe began checking on Pesto and eventually kept a close eye on her at all times.

"It was almost like Abe had a job again," says Hyman. "That thrilled him! After a year his feet completely healed. He also got a bright look back in his eyes again. More than three years after we first got him, he is happy and healthy. He still spends his days minding Pesto."

Abe is the perfect example of a rescued horse that could not be put up for adoption but still enjoys a wonderful life at a sanctuary. He was unwanted and headed toward an early death. Rescue workers saved him and helped prove that even horses that are old and sick can thrive when given a second chance.

Abe (left) is great friends with Pesto (right) at SquirrelWood.

The Perfect Polo Horse

Parchita made her way to SquirrelWood in March 2009. She was about fifteen years old at the time and, like Abe, had not had an easy life. Parchita was a former polo horse. Polo is a sport that is similar to field hockey. Unlike field hockey, however, polo is played on horseback by athletes using long-handled mallets and a wooden ball.

Yet Parchita looked very little like a proud polo champion when Hyman found her. Like Abe, she was also being auctioned off in New Holland. Parchita was in terrible shape. She was filthy and covered in manure. Parchita had a bad infection, too.

"We got her home after the auction and began treating her [infection]," Hyman says. "It took almost a month to see any changes . . . . We cleaned her up and gave her good feed. She began to feel better, and her coat began to shine." It grew clear that Parchita could eventually be put up for adoption. She was well behaved and in good health after the workers at SquirrelWood spent time caring for her. After a while, Hyman mentioned Parchita's story to a friend she played indoor polo with during the winter months. She even offered to let her friend use the polo horse when he played over the summer. Hyman's friend agreed to take Parchita home with him.

Everyone was pleased to see that Parchita still enjoyed playing the game. Even though she had been through a lot, she had stayed speedy and was easy to ride. Eventually, a man from Virginia saw Parchita playing polo and fell in love with her. SquirrelWood carefully interviewed him and finally arranged for him to adopt the horse. According to Hyman, Parchita is now living with her new owner in Virginia and plays polo for a few months every year.

Parchita is a good example of a rescued horse that ended up being placed in a new home. Her story before being rescued was sad, but her life became more hopeful and happy thanks to rescue workers. Today, Parchita is playing a game she enjoys with an owner who loves her.

How People Can Do Their Part

Maybe you are not ready to open your own rescue or sanctuary. Yet this does not mean that you cannot help the unwanted horses that end up there. All people, from lawmakers to kids like you, can help change the lives of these amazing animals.

Volunteers exercise Autumn (left) and Goliath (right) at the Whimsical Equine Rescue.

For example, more states are passing laws to make sure that horses are not abandoned or neglected when they can no longer race or do certain jobs. Some lawmakers are also trying to create programs that retrain horses to do new kinds of activities if they are unable to continue doing the same kind of work.

Sponsor a Special Animal!

Perhaps you are not prepared to adopt a horse this very second. You can still sponsor a rescued horse, though. Sponsoring an animal usually involves donating a little money every year to help pay for its care. Rescued horses often have more than one sponsor at a time. This allows rescues and sanctuaries to use extra money to take in new animals that are in danger of being slaughtered. Think about calling a local horse-rescue group in your area to see if it might let you sponsor a horse. Some rescues and sanctuaries may even allow you to visit your special animal.

Many rescues and sanctuaries say that adoption is another way people can help unwanted horses. Adoption is sometimes cheaper than buying a horse from a breeder. Owners who adopt are saving lives as well. They open up available spots for new horses that might otherwise face neglect, abuse, or death.

What can you do to help rescued horses? Think about visiting a rescue or sanctuary with your friends so you can learn more. Plan events at your school to raise money to donate to these organizations. Abe and Parchita are proof that every horse deserves the second chance that rescues and sanctuaries can give them.

Glossary

aggressive Ready to fight or attack.

auction To sell goods or animals to the highest bidder.

corrals Pens where farm animals are kept.

euthanized Put to death in a humane way.

feedlots Areas where farm animals are housed and fed before being sent to slaughter.

grazing Putting cattle or other farm animals in a field to feed on grass.

groomed Cleaned and brushed.

herd A large group of animals that live together.

lame Crippled or unable to move normally.

paddock A small field or pen where horses are kept.

quarantine An area where animals are kept until people are sure they will not spread any illnesses.

rehabilitated Given treatment to recover from a physical or emotional problem.

sanctuaries Shelters that take in unwanted horses and often care for them for the rest of their lives.

screen To test someone to see if he or she is fit for a certain job or responsibility.

slaughterhouse A place where animals are killed for food or other products.

Find Out More

Books

Kummer, Patricia K. *Working Horses*. New York: Cavendish Square, 2014.

Ledu, Stéphanie, and Cécile Hudrisier (illustrator). *The Horse Lover's Book*. San Anselmo, CA: Treasure Bay, 2008.

Trueit, Trudi Strain. *Horse Care*. New York: Cavendish Square, 2014.

DVD

Black Beauty. Warner Brothers Pictures, 1994.

Websites

**The Humane Society of the United States (HSUS)—
Homeless Horses**

www.humanesociety.org/issues/homeless_horses/
This page discusses what happens to homeless horses and includes several videos related to horse rescue.

SquirrelWood Equine Sanctuary

www.squirrelwoodequinesanctuaryinc.org/
This site features details about the sanctuary and highlights different issues connected to horse rescue.

Index

Page numbers in **boldface** are illustrations.

About the Author

Katie Marsico lives in Elmhurst, Illinois, with her husband and children. Marsico graduated from the Medill School of Journalism at Northwestern University in Evanston, Illinois. She worked as an editor in children's publishing before authoring more than one hundred books for young people.